A New True Book

COWBOYS

By Teri Martini

This "true book" was prepared
under the direction of
Illa Podendorf,
formerly with the Laboratory School,
University of Chicago

CHILDRENS PRESS, CHICAGO

PHOTO CREDITS

© 1981 James Fain, Logan, Utah—cover, 2, 7, 13, 17, 19 (bottom), 23, 24 (4 photos), 28, 29, 32, 34, 41, 44 (top), 45

Texas State Department of Highways and Public Transportation—4, 8, 10 (2 photos), 12, 14, 15, 19 (2 photos at top), 21, 35, 38, 42, 44 (bottom)

Bobbie Lieberman, Equus Magazine—26 (above)

John McDonald, Equus Magazine—26 (below)

Randy Huffman, Crockett, Texas—30, 33 (2 photos), 40

United States Department of Agriculture—37

Cover—Cattle Drive, Utah

Library of Congress Cataloging in Publication Data

Martini, Teri.
  Cowboys.

  (A New true book)
  Rev. ed. of: The true book of Cowboys.
  SUMMARY: Briefly describes the clothing
cowboys wear; their duties on the ranch,
range, and roundup; and their recreation at
rodeos.
  1. Cowboys—Juvenile literature.   2. West
(U.S.)—Social life and customs—Juvenile
literature.   3. Ranch life—West (U.S.)—
Juvenile literature. [1. Cowboys]   I. Title.
F596.M33 1981   978   81-10049
ISBN 0-516-01611-3   AACR2

TABLE OF CONTENTS

COWBOYS AND THEIR HORSES

Cowboys take care of cattle. The cowboys work on ranches.

Often the cattle ranch has miles and miles of open land. This is the range. The cattle wander far to find grass.

For hundreds of years the cowboys and their horses have looked after cattle.

Today there are not many cowboys. And machines do some of a cowboy's work. But cowboys and their horses still are needed.

SPRING ROUND-UP

Today the cowboys get up early. It is time for the spring round-up.

Each cowboy has a horse. He keeps the horse in a corral or barn.

But there are other horses on the ranch. They wander with the cattle.

The cowboys saddle up their horses. They ride out to find the other horses. They bring them back to the corral.

Cowboys
eat well
before
round-up.

The next morning the cowboys start the round-up.

The cowboys take along the extra horses. The horses are needed for the round-up.

Saddling up the horses

Taking a break on the range

During the round-up the
cowboys live outside. They
ride all day to the place
where they will camp. They
get their supper. Then they
go to sleep under the
stars.

One of the cowboys is always awake. He is called the nighthawk.

The next morning the cowboys ride "circle." This means they ride off in a wide circle to look for the cattle.

A cowboy finds some cows with calves. He rides around them. He waves his hat. This is called hazing. This is the way he drives them into camp.

Sometimes cowboys use aircraft to find the cattle.

The cowboys know their cattle by the mark or brand on the side. The brand shows who owns the cattle. It takes a few days to find them. When all the cattle are in camp, the calves are branded. They also are given medicine. This helps keep them well.

BRANDING THE CALVES

A cowboy rides in between the calf and its mother. This is called cutting out the calves. A lasso drops over the calf's head. The horse stands still and holds the rope tight.

The cowboy jumps down. He ties three of the calf's legs together. Another cowboy touches the calf's side with a hot iron. The calf is branded.

Then the calf jumps up. It runs off to find its mother.

At last all the calves are branded. The cattle are turned loose again. So are the extra horses. Then the cowboys ride for home.

Cowboys going home

A cowboy and his dog look after the cattle. The horses get looked after, too. The cowboy at lower right looks at his horse's hoofs. The cowboy below is shaping a new horseshoe.

SUMMER ON THE RANCH

In summer there is much work for the cowboys. Some go on the range to watch the cattle. Some mend fences. Others train horses.

The young horses are called yearlings. In summer they are brought in off the range. Cowboys work with the yearlings. Soon they become used to people. When they are older they will learn to carry a rider.

Bull riding

RODEOS

Cowboys do not work all of the time. One of the things they do for fun is go to the rodeo. The best cowboys enter contests.

Calf roping

There is calf roping. The winner ropes a calf and ties its legs in the shortest time.

There is bulldogging. The cowboy throws a steer off its feet by twisting its horns.

Some of the cowboys
ride bucking broncos.
Some ride Brahma bulls.

Rodeos once were just a
fun time for cowboys. Now
some cowboys don't work
on ranches anymore. They
go to rodeos to win money
and prizes.

FALL ROUND-UP

Fall comes. It is round-up time again.

This time full-grown cattle are rounded up. They are driven to a feed lot. They are put on trucks by the people who buy them.

The cattle are healthy.
They bring a good price.
The cowboys have done
their work well.

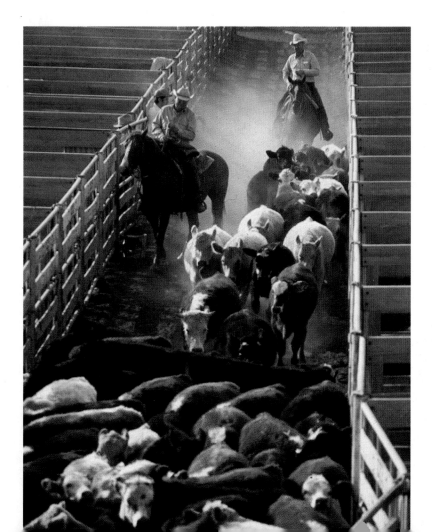

WINTER ON THE RANGE

In winter, the cowboys look after the cattle still on the range. They give the cattle salt. When it snows the cattle can't eat grass. So the cowboys take the cattle hay to eat.

COWBOY CLOTHES

A cowboy's clothes are good clothes for the work he does. His big hat shades his eyes. It helps keep his head cool. And he can use it to wave at cattle who are trying to run away.

Boots help cowboys keep their feet in the stirrups.

A stirrup

Cowboy boots have small tips and high heels. The tips let the boots fit into a stirrup easily. The heels keep the boots from slipping. The boots' leather sides protect a cowboy from snake bites.

Sometimes he also wears leather pants legs. These are chaps. They protect his legs from sharp bushes.

He needs a warm shirt. He is outside a lot.

Cowboys work hard all year round. They take care of cattle. They take care of the ranch. And their rodeos are for fun.

WORDS YOU SHOULD KNOW

Brahma (BRAH • muh) — a kind of bull

brand — a mark burned into an animal's skin to show who owns it

bucking bronco (BUHK • ing BRONK • oh) — a horse that jumps upward and forward

bull-dogging — to throw an animal to the ground by grabbing the horns and twisting the head

calf (KAF) — a young cow or bull

chaps — heavy leather pants without a seat that are put over regular pants to protect the legs

corral (kuh • RALL) — an area with a fence around it where animals are kept

cutting out — to ride a horse between a calf and its mother so as to separate them

haze (HAYZ) — to drive cattle back into their camp by making loud noises and waving things at them

lasso (LASS • oh) — a long rope with a loop at one end used to catch animals

nighthawk — the cowboy who stays awake and watches at night

range (RAYNJ) — a large, open area of land where animals feed on the plants

rodeo (ROH • dee • oh) — a show where cowboys enter contests like cattle roping, bronco riding, and other events

round-up — to gather animals together

yearling (YEER • ling) — an animal in its second year

INDEX

About the Author

Teri Martini is a teacher turned writer. Her titles in the True Book series grew out of specific needs she saw in her elementary school classrooms. She has a Masters Degree in education from Columbia University. Among the 22 books she has written, 14 are for children. Her short stories and articles have appeared in Scott Foresman Basic Readers, Childcraft, Scholastic Publications, and 'Teen Magazine. At present she divides her time between writing and teaching other writers to write for children through The Institute of Children's Literature in Redding Ridge, Connecticut. She is listed in Who's Who of American Women, Contemporary Authors and The International Dictionary of Biography.